How do I use this scheme?

Key Words with Peter and Jane has three
parallel series, each containing twelve books. All three
series are written using the same carefully controlled
vocabulary. Readers will get the most out of **Key Words** with
Peter and Jane when they follow the books in the pattern
1a, 1b, 1c; 2a, 2b, 2c and so on.

• Series a
gradually introduces and repeats new words.

• Series b
provides further practice of these same words, but
in a different context and with different illustrations.

• Series c
uses familiar words to teach **phonics** in a methodical way,
enabling children to read increasingly difficult words.
It also provides a link to writing.

LADYBIRD BOOKS

UK | USA | Canada | Ireland | Australia
India | New Zealand | South Africa

Ladybird Books is part of the Penguin Random House group of companies
whose addresses can be found at global.penguinrandomhouse.com.

www.penguin.co.uk   www.puffin.co.uk   www.ladybird.co.uk

First published 1964
This edition 2009, 2014, 2016
Copyright © Ladybird Books Ltd, 1964
001

A CIP catalogue record for this book is
available from the British Library

ISBN: 978-1-409-30119-6

Printed in China

Key Words

with Peter and Jane

3c

Let me write

written by W. Murray
illustrated by M. Aitchison

After reading Books 3a and 3b the learner should copy out and complete the following pages in an exercise book. Answers are given on Pages 46 to 51 for corrections, revision and testing.

1 I see a b--.

2 I see a g---.

3 I see a d--.

4 I see a r-----.

The answers are on Page 46

a boy

a girl

a dog

a rabbit

1 Give me some s-----.

2 Give me some c----.

3 Give me some a-----.

4 Give me some f------.

The answers are on Page 46

sweets

cakes

apples

flowers

1 We can see P————.

2 We can see J———.

3 We can see D————.

4 We can see M————.

Peter	Jane
Daddy	Mummy

The answers are on Page 46

1 Look at the b--.

2 Look at the b---.

3 Look at the c--.

4 Look at the b--.

The answers are on Page 47

1 he bus

2 the boat

3 the car

4 the bed

1 I want to play
  with the b‒‒‒.

2 I want to play
  with the d‒‒.

3 I want to play
  with the t‒‒‒‒.

4 I want to play
  with the r‒‒‒‒‒.

The answers are on Page 47

the ball

the dog

the train

the rabbit

1 Here comes P————.

2 Here comes J———.

3 Here comes M————.

4 Here comes D————.

Peter Jane Mummy Daddy

The answers are on Page 47

1 Jane helps Mummy
with the c————.

2 Peter helps Daddy
with the c——.

3 Jane helps Mummy
with the f——————.

4 Peter helps Daddy
with the b———.

cakes   car   flowers   boat

The answers are on Page 47

1 The man is in the b--.

2 The boy is in the t---.

3 The dog is in the w----

4 The girl is in the t----.

| bus | tree |
| water | train |

The answers are on Page 48

up   down

1 Help me -- , says Peter

2 The dog jumps ----.

3 Jane looks --.

4 Daddy comes ----.

The answers are on Page 48

1 Give me a– apple, pleas‑

2 Give me some t– –, pleas‑

3 Here is o– – red ball.

4 The boy and the girl
  go to this s– – – – –.

an apple	some tea
one ball	school

The answers are on Page 48

1 This man is in the P-----

2 Here is the Police S------

3 It is a P------ car.

4 The Police h--- you.

Police   Station   help

The answers are on Page 48

1 Daddy and Peter get int
the b---.

2 Peter likes fun in the boc
with D----.

3 He wants to f---.

4 They see a fish j---.

boat	Daddy
fish	jump

The answers are on Page 49

1 Jane has a shop at home

2 Jane has tea and cakes
in the s---.

3 Peter has some t--
in the shop.

4 That was good, he s---.
It was g--- tea, Jane.

shop	tea
says	good

The answers are on Page 49

Jane's teashop

Yes   No

1 Are apples good
  for you? ---.

2 Have Peter and Jane
  some toys? ---.

3 Can you write? ---.

4 Can Pat write? --.

The answers are on Page 49

I can write

Yes   No

1 Is the rabbit red? --.

2 Can you see Jane
in bed? --.

3 Can you see the bus?---

4 Can you see apples
on the tree? ---.

The answers are on Page 49

1

2

3

4

Write out each sentence correctly,
choosing the missing word from
those given in brackets.

1 Peter says he is in the
(please Police plays).

2 The boy and the girl loo
at the (tea tree train).

3 Jane says, Please get me
an (ball apple sweet).

4 Peter says, That was
(give girl good).

The answers are on Page 50

3

2

1

4

1 Jane and Peter want to
get on the (bus boat bed

2 They want to go to
(school apples some).

3 The school bus is
(says red good).

4 On the bus are boys and
(gives girls fish).

The answers are on Page 50

1 We want to go to the station, please, says Pete to (rabbit Daddy Police

2 Peter and Jane like it at the (water comes station

3 The train is in the (station school shop).

4 They want to get into th (this train play).

The answers are on Page 50

Write out correctly—

1 Peter says, Police a car
That was.

2 down Jane and jumps up

3 Jane says, An me apple
for and you for apple ar

4 Peter says, that is Yes m
one for and you one for.

The answers are on Page 51

Write out correctly—

1 Jane Mummy for flowers cakes and gets.

2 The bed the boy on is.

3 Peter rabbit the with play

4 a car red in a man is Her

The answers are on Page 51

Write out correctly—

1 Mummy water some flowers the gives.

2 Mummy Jane to help wants.

3 Peter Pat with wants to up get.

4 up here Peter I like it say

The answers are on Page 51

Pages 46 to 51 give answers to the written exercises in this book. They can also be used for revision and testing, before proceeding to Book 4a.

Page 4
1   I see a boy.
2   I see a girl.
3   I see a dog.
4   I see a rabbit.

Page 6
1   Give me some sweets.
2   Give me some cakes.
3   Give me some apples.
4   Give me some flowers.

Page 8
1   We can see Peter.
2   We can see Jane.
3   We can see Daddy.
4   We can see Mummy.

Answers

Page 10

1 Look at the bus.

2 Look at the boat.

3 Look at the car.

4 Look at the bed.

Page 12

1 I want to play with the ball.

2 I want to play with the dog.

3 I want to play with the train.

4 I want to play with the rabbit.

Page 14

1 Here comes Peter.

2 Here comes Jane.

3 Here comes Mummy.

4 Here comes Daddy.

Page 16

1 Jane helps Mummy with the cakes.

2 Peter helps Daddy with the car.

3 Jane helps Mummy with the flowers.

4 Peter helps Daddy with the boat.

Answers

Page 18

1   The man is in the bus.
2   The boy is in the tree.
3   The dog is in the water.
4   The girl is in the train.

Page 20

1   Help me up, says Peter.
2   The dog jumps down.
3   Jane looks up.
4   Daddy comes down.

Page 22

1   Give me an apple, please.
2   Give me some tea, please.
3   Here is one red ball.
4   The boy and the girl go to this school.

Page 24

1   This man is in the Police.
2   Here is the Police Station.
3   It is a Police car.
4   The Police help you.

Answers

Page 26

1   Daddy and Peter get into the boat.
2   Peter likes fun in the boat with Daddy.
3   He wants to fish.
4   They see a fish jump.

Page 28

1   Jane has a shop at home.
2   Jane has tea and cakes in the shop.
3   Peter has some tea in the shop.
4   That was good, he says.
    It was good tea, Jane.

Page 30

1   Are apples good for you? Yes.
2   Have Peter and Jane some toys? Yes.
3   Can you write? Yes.
4   Can Pat write? No.

Page 32

1   Is the rabbit red? No.
2   Can you see Jane in bed? No.
3   Can you see the bus? Yes.
4   Can you see apples on the tree? Yes.

Answers

Page 34

1 Peter says he is in the Police.

2 The boy and the girl look at the train.

3 Jane says, Please get me an apple.

4 Peter says, That was good.

Page 36

1 Jane and Peter want to get on the bus.

2 They want to go to school.

3 The school bus is red.

4 On the bus are boys and girls.

Page 38

1 We want to go to the station, please, says Peter to Daddy.

2 Peter and Jane like it at the station.

3 The train is in the station.

4 They want to get into the train.

Answers

Page 40

1 Peter says, That was a Police car.

2 Jane jumps up and down.

3 Jane says, An apple for you and an apple for me .

4 Peter says, Yes, that is one for you and one for me .

Page 42

1 Jane gets cakes and flowers for Mummy.

2 The boy is on the bed.

3 Peter plays with the rabbit.

4 Here is a man in a red car.

Page 44

1 Mummy gives the flowers some water.

2 Jane wants to help Mummy.

3 Pat wants to get up with Peter.

4 Peter says, I like it up here.

New words used in this book

Total number of new words: 36
This book provides the link with writing for
the words in Readers 3a and 3b.